America, America

*America, America,
God shed His grace on thee,
And crowned thy good
with brotherhood,
From sea to shining sea.*

AMERICA, AMERICA
ISBN 1-878859-13-7
Library of Congress Card # 94-92338
Non-copyright September, 1994
Living Waters Publications
P.O. Box 1172
Bellflower
CA 90706

Cover design Harry Brut & Erik Hollander

Printed in the United States

Any portion of this book *may* be copied, reproduced, stored, transmitted or photocopied in part or in full, without written permission from the publisher.

This publication is available at a special bulk-rate price. See page 121 for details.

Foreword

It was the French King, Louis the 17th, who uttered the memorable last words as he passed from this life in 1795, "*I have something to tell you...*" leaving his hearers dying to know what he was about to say. I also have something to tell you, but I intend to finish what I begin.

However, after starting to write about the troubles of America, I began asking myself if I had the right, as a legal alien, to speak to Americans on such a sensitive subject. I had no peace, so I made the project a matter of prayer.

Sometime earlier, someone had given me a set of books of sermons by a preacher of the last century. When I began reading a page from a sermon each day, my youngest son calculated that I would finish the volumes in 50 years.

Around the time I prayed, I picked up a one hundred-year-old sermon (preached in England) and read the following words:

"Seeking the good of the country as aliens, we must also remember that it behoves aliens to keep themselves very quiet. What business have foreigners to plot against the government in which they have no citizenship? He will be injudicious indeed, if he cannot leave America to the Americans."

So, I am now an American citizen, and as an American I can talk to Americans about America...I hope you will listen.

Contents

Chapter 1. Pick the Odd One -- 9
Chapter 2. Drink and Live -- 25
Chapter 3. What's Going On? -- 35
Chapter 4. Let's Personalize -- 51
Chapter 5. The Judgment of Sin City -- 57
Chapter 6. Creating Havoc -- 81
Chapter 7. Let Lying Dogs Sleep -- 89
Chapter 8. Fixing the Feet -- 103
Chapter 9. Fish With Fancy Fins -- 115

Dedication: To my friend and computer genius, Daniel Ho.

Chapter One
Pick the Odd One

In 1983, in Bogota, Colombia, a mother rushed Jensen, her 10-month-old baby who had an acute case of diarrhea, to a hospital near her village. When she came to get her baby the next day, his eyes were bandaged and he was covered with splotches of blood. Horrified, she asked what was wrong with the boy, and was dismissed coldly by a doctor who told her that the child was dying.

In a panic, she raced Jensen to another doctor who examined his wounds and said, *"They've stolen his eyes!"*

The baby was the victim of "organ-napping," where eyeballs are removed and the corneas sold on the black market. In one sense Jensen was

America America

fortunate--most victims are murdered.

In the early 60's, when the Ten Commandments were removed from the schools of the United States, authorities removed the eyes from an entire generation. The "Commandment is a lamp, and the Law is light," and removal of the Law left a generation in the dark as to moral absolutes. We now live at a time when a breed of human beings can kill, steal, lie, hate, dishonor their parents, and hate God without qualms of conscience.

In June of 1993, six teenaged gang members in northwest Houston, raped and killed two girls aged 14 and 16 years. The leader of the gang, Peter Cantu (19), boasted how he and other members abducted two young girls, raped and sodomized them before strangling them. According to their testimony in court, "It took a while for them to die." They strangled one girl with a belt until it broke, kicking her in the mouth and knocking out three of her teeth with a steel boot, and strangled the other with a shoe lace. They then took turns stomping on their necks to make sure they died. These heinous crimes are all too common in our lawless society.

The MTV generation doesn't lack the moral values of its grandparents, it doesn't have *any* moral values. In previous years, there was a "moral" code even among criminals, that when

America America

you stole from someone, you didn't blast them with your gun as you left. Not so nowadays. We are daily reminded that what one generation permits, they next embraces as normality. Years ago, a woman would hesitate to walk in front of a group of men for a concern that they would take her clothes off with their eyes. Nowadays, her fear is that she will be raped, sodomized and murdered.

Intelligence Test

See if you can pick the odd one out: earthquakes, floods, droughts, cancer, AIDS, tuberculosis, hurricanes, God's blessing, tornadoes, killer bees.

Of course "God's blessing" is the oddity. Yet, there are many who would believe the entire list is harmonious. In their ignorance, they think that the devastating things that are happening to this nation, are nothing more than nature doing her own thing.

You may have noticed that lately there has been an increase in Mother Nature's rumblings. In fact, nine of the most expensive disasters in U.S. history happened in the five years from 1989 to 1994. You may also be aware that in the last ten years, incidents of cancer in the U.S. have increased *three-fold*. That means there is a

America America

300% more chance of getting cancer than there was ten years ago. In just over one ten-year period, 160,000 people died of AIDS, but during the same time span (1981-1994) 330,000 men died of prostate cancer. The disease strikes one man in eleven, and will kill over 34,000 in the next 12 months. One woman in ten develops breast cancer, with 180,000 new cases each year, and 150,000 new cases of colon cancer yearly (*U.S. News & World Report*, Aug '94).

Cancer isn't our only dilemma. Back in 1993, Americans spent an incredible $898 *billion* on health care. We have moved from one of the lowest infant mortality rates to one of the highest, with over 40,000 newborns dying each year. In one year 52,000 were killed by a flu virus. The National Alliance for Mental Illness diagnosed that 10 million people have serious long-term mental disease, and over 37,000,000 Americans have arthritis. The U.S. at present is plagued by killer earthquakes, new incurable diseases that are out-witting anti-biotics, the return of once "conquered" diseases such as tuberculosis, killer hurricanes, devastating tornadoes, calamitous floods, terrible droughts, and the invasion of killer bees, just to name a few.

Moral Measure

The Scriptures tell us that "righteousness

America America

exalts a nation, but sin is a reproach to any people." Let's see how we are doing morally:

1. **Adultery** (50-60% of married couples admit to committing adultery. In California alone, 500,000 couples "live together").
2. **Fornication** (every day 33,000 teens get some sort of sexually transmitted disease. Each year over 800,000 babies are born to unwed teenagers. A 1990 survey found that 40% of school children had had at least three sexual partners).
3. **Rape** (each year over 120,000 women report being raped; 5,000 are killed by domestic violence. According to a Justice Department survey, children are beaten, raped, and robbed five times more than adults. On average, 1 in 13 will be raped).
4. **Pornography** (a $32,000,000,000 industry).
5. **Abortion** (1,500,000 annually, 146,000 done in the third trimester).
6. **Theft** (3,000,000 burglaries annually. One Chicago department store reported $22,000,000 in shoplifting in one year, with a national annual 140,000,000 shoplifting offenses. 1.8 billion dollars worth of food stamps were received by people who were not entitled to them in 1993. One government official said that the amount

America America

was an underestimate of "the tremendous amount of fraud in the food stamp program." According to CNN, the U.S. loses $150,000,000,000 each year through tax cheating. Crime costs $500,000,000,000 each year).

7. Greed (over $240,000,000,000 was spent on gambling in one year).

8. Murder (over 24,000 people are murdered annually; 40,000,000 are the victims of violent crime. The number one killer of children is parents. Over 1600 people are murdered each year while "on the job." I met with a group of pastors recently in Long Beach. One of the pastors held up a local newspaper with the pictures of 36 people around the edge of the front page. They were the photographs of 36 victims who had been murdered within a 2 square mile area of where the pastors churches were based. The pictures brought a sense of reality to the fact that these murdered people weren't just statistics, they were fathers, mothers, sons and daughters).

9. Drunkenness (90,000,000 cans of beer are sold each day, and our roads have become slaughterhouses for drunk drivers, who are killing over 25,000 people yearly).

10. Hypocrisy (62% profess to be Christians; 91% lie regularly).

America America

We don't seem to be doing too well. We are no different than Israel, who through the ages, kept straying from God's Commandments into lawlessness. From there they lost the promised blessings of health, which were conditional upon her righteousness (Deuteronomy 28:15-46).

The Blessings
Take the time to study how wonderfully God promises to bless Israel if they walk in obedience. The opening verses in the passage say that their children would be born healthy and stay healthy. Can you imagine having children who are free from leukemia, cerebral palsy, down syndrome, asthma, sudden infant death syndrome and the thousands of other diseases that bring misery to millions? Can you picture having the rain come in its season, watering pestilence-free golden crops, and fruit trees which bulge with harvest? The soil would furnish its yield with the ease that it normally produces weeds. When Israel was obedient, God gave them prosperity beyond their wildest dreams, as in the case of King Solomon.

The Bible shows what it was like under God's blessing:

"You visit the earth and water it, You greatly

America America

enrich it; the river of God is full of water; You provide their grain, for so You have prepared it...You crown the year with Your goodness, and Your paths drip with abundance...the pastures are clothed with flocks; the valleys are also covered with grain; they shout for joy, they also sing... He causes the grass to grow for the cattle, and vegetation for the service of man, that he may bring forth fruit from the earth, and wine that makes glad the heart of man, oil to make his face shine, and bread which strengthens man's heart" (Psalm 65:9-13, 104:14-23).

The thing that shines here, is the harmony of all of creation. The heavens water the earth, the sun warms it, the soil yields its harvest, the animals eat, and man rejoices. The Apostle Paul said of God, "He...gave us rain from heaven and fruitful seasons, filling our heart with food and gladness" (Acts 14:17). Then the psalmist speaks of the oil that makes the machinery of creation work:

"These all wait for You, that You may give them their food in due season. What You give them they gather in; You open Your hand, they are filled with good. You hide Your face,

America America

they are troubled; You take away their breath, they die and return to their dust" (Psalm 104:27-29).

While we may be of the impression that God remains in Heaven, He is in fact omnipresent, and fills His creation as the waters fill the sea-- "In Him we live and move and have our being." Not a sparrow falls without God falling with it. Not a hair on our head grows without having its very atoms exposed before His eyes. As much as the world would love it to be so, God is not afar off, ignorant, dispassionate and uninvolved in the affairs of mankind. The Bible says, "His judgments are in the earth" (Psalm 105:7):

"...for when Your judgments are in the earth, *the inhabitants of the world will learn righteousness*" (Isaiah 26:9b, italics added).

Tornadoes, hurricanes, floods, and earthquakes, etc., should make us remember that God is righteous. They should make us see that He is not pleased with our murderous ways, and examine our own hearts in the light of His Word.

It was Patrick Henry, the man who uttered "Give me liberty, or give me death," who rightly

America America

said, "There is a just God who presides over the destinies of nations."

Benjamin Franklin, when speaking with George Washington said,

"I have lived, sir, a long time, and the longer I live, the more convincing proofs I see of this truth: 'That God governs in the affairs of man.' And if a sparrow cannot fall to the ground without His notice, is it probable that an empire can rise without His aid?"

Out of Sight

If lightning strikes your house and it burns to the ground, or if an earthquake destroys your property, the insurance company will usually call the incident an "act of God." We give Mother Nature thanks for the sunset, the flowers, the birds and trees, and we blame God for disasters. The world calls a natural disaster an "act of God," but if a *Christian* points to a destructive flood, or a killer earthquake, and even hints that it could possibly be an *act of God*, he is labeled a fanatic. They are offended because a genuine act of God speaks of blame and responsibility, something the world would rather not face because they suffer from chronic BDS--*Blame Deficiency Syndrome*.

America America

The Scriptures tell us how the ungodly think:

"God is in none of his thoughts…Your judgments are far above, out of his sight" (Psalm 10:4-5).

Darwinism brain-washing has left the world with the misconception that a remote God (who perhaps was responsible for evolution) smiles, no matter what is happening on earth. The skies fire arrows of lightning and burn him, the ground opens its mouth wide and swallows him with earthquakes, the animals devour him, disease eats his flesh, and still his thoroughly rinsed brain thinks he is weighed in the balance and sits pretty.

Consider for a moment the things that bug you in this life (and ask yourself if God had anything to do with creating these distressing annoyances): It's a hot night. You can't sleep because it's so humid. Besides, there is a mosquito in your bedroom and it woke you up with an aggravating buzzing around your ear hole. It must have been a victory dance because it bit you on the face, and now its poison has given you a hot itchy cheek which is adding to your insomnia. One consolation is that you were having a nightmare anyway.

America America

Unbeknown to you, there is a disease-infested cockroach rubbing its dirty little legs together on the dresser not far from your head. Its beady eyes can penetrate the dark and see a spider slowly lowering its ugly self by its web directly above your head. As you lay on your back, you yawn widely and breath in the hot bedroom air.

In the still of the dark night you think of the jobs you have to do tomorrow. You want to make time to spray the fruit trees with a pesticide, to get rid of the grubs that are burrowing through your peaches, and to keep the blight off your apples. Then you have to make a scarecrow to keep the birds away from the fruit that the grubs haven't yet eaten.

There seems to be no way you can stop the rats from consuming your avocadoes. You have helplessly witnessed them run along the power lines and drop onto the tree at night. Speaking of the rat family--you will have to crawl into the attic and put out some poison for the mice you can hear scratching and scampering through your walls at night. The poison may also kill the infestation of roaches that you suspect may be there. You want to stop them before they get into your bedroom. Remember what the commercial says, "If you have seen one, there are hundreds more."

America America

That thought reminds you--you must replace that rotten wood on the garage roof. The termites must have made it their home last year and eaten the wood. It is so rotten, you can poke your finger right through it. More than likely, you will have to call the experts to fumigate the garage and the whole house. The neighbor should get his house done too. You've noticed wasps flying in and out of his roof.

Fumigation might also slow down the plague of ants that find the smallest amount of food on the kitchen counter each morning. Speaking of plagues--the dog needs another flea dip; not that that works. The fleas must have infected the carpet. The kids are covered in bites. The yard probably needs another spraying with more pesticide to kill their eggs. Besides that, the animal needs another rabies shot.

With all these plans, how are you going to get time to weed the garden as you planned? The weeds seem to shoot up from nowhere. If only the vegetables grew with such energy! Imagine. Why is it that the white butterflies eat the cabbages and other vegetables, and leave the weeds?

No wonder you can't sleep with all these things on your mind. As if you haven't enough problems with the extra labor at work--the foreman's wife having cancer has taken his time

America America

and added to your load. There seems to be a lot of that about. At least his problems dwarf yours--your continual painful mouth ulcers...and the headaches your wife is getting. It could be the spray she is using to try and get rid of the persistent mildew in the bathroom; you told her to make sure she had good ventilation by opening a window. You also must remind her that the kids are due for their shots for rubella, measles, Hepatitis B and those other diseases.

For Our Attention

Think of it this way, if God did create everything as we know it, then didn't He bungle things? Or perhaps you think He designed the disease-infested mosquito as a practical joke, and that cancer, and earthquakes, etc., are some sort of strange blessing. The alternative to blind conjecture, is to open the Bible and humbly let the light of God's word reveal the truth to you.

We can't be sure if God's hand is in a particular incident. Those who understand the principles of God's judgments can't help but look to the heavens, when torrents of rain pour from the skies causing the Mississippi river to rush south at 1 million cubic feet per second. We wonder if God is saying something when it surges over its banks, floods 6.6 million acres, takes 38 lives, destroys $12 billion in homes and crops and strands $1.6 billion worth of waterborne cargo. We can't be positive that when world oil prices drop, drying up local markets in America, that God is involved, but we must remember that God says He *will* bring judgment to the nations and bring them to nothing. Scripture tells us that "the king's heart is in the hand of the Lord, like the rivers of water; He turns it wherever He wishes" (Prov. 21:1). We are told that "He rules over the nations" (Psalm 22:28), "He makes nations great, and destroys them..." (Job 12:23).

When nations "rage" and cast off the restraints of godly influence, the Bible tells us that God will "distress them in His deep displeasure" (Psalm 2:1-5). He puts them "in fear," that they "may know themselves to be but men" (Psalm 9:20).

So, to come to the conclusion that America is somehow insulated from Divine wrath, that God has confined His judgments to Israel and her surrounding nations, or has restricted them to biblical times, is inconsistent with Divine revelation.

The Scriptures tell us, "Blessed is the nation whose God is the Lord" (Psalm 33:12). The United States at present cannot say it's being blessed by God, so it seems obvious that (al-

America America

though there is an acknowledgement of God), He isn't "Lord" of the nation. The Word of God tells us that He sent mildew, blight, and plagues, etc., to get a nation's attention. It took ten plagues to bring Pharaoh to his knees. Let's hope America isn't so stubborn.

Chapter Two
Drink and Live

Here now are the afflictions that God said would come upon Israel if they turned their backs on His Law (it doesn't take a social genius to see a similarity between modern America and sinful Israel):

1. They would be cursed in the city (Deuteronomy 28:16). America's cities have become infamous for their murder, rape, drugs, pornography, and organized crime. The United States cities are filled with people who are gripped with the fear of crime. More and more people are arming themselves, with over 216,000,000 firearms in the hands of citizens, double the total in 1970.

Our cities should be a place of safety in which we can raise our families, but instead they

America America

have become a curse to the nation.

Rats (of the four legged kind) are invading many cities and bringing the usual accompanying diseases. Authorities in L.A. have called their infestation a "serious epidemic," with the pest control business up by 50%. Experts say that they don't expect the invasion to end soon, blaming the previous year's rain, creating more food as the probable cause.

Meanwhile, across town, the city of Huntington Beach would probably gladly have an exchange program. The problem of an infestation of skunks is so high on their agenda, the locals called a special town council meeting. The council said that they had officers who were equipped to handle mountain lions, bears, snakes and other deadly creatures (who have also been assailing Southern California), but they had no way of dealing with the skunks.

One of the judgments upon Israel for her sins was that God would send wild animals into her midst (Leviticus 26:22).

2. They would be cursed in their fields (verse 16). Farming was once the backbone of the United States but the backbone has crumbled under the weight of financial debt, drought, floods and pestilence. In fact, things have been so bad, rock concerts called "Farm Aid" have

America America

been held to raise money to keep farmers in business.

3. Their children would be cursed (verse 18). America's children are victims of child abuse, rape, drugs and alcohol. One in twenty young girls is the victim of incest, while suicides among teenagers is at an all time high. One in 13 will be raped, and it has become commonplace for children to be kidnapped and sexually abused or used as child prostitutes. I don't know about you, but I am tired of seeing the heart-reding sight of mothers and fathers weeping over their murdered children. Over 5,300 children were killed by guns in a single year.

The Census Bureau revealed that in 1994, 18 million children (more than one in five children) are growing up with only one parent, twice as many as in 1970. While a single parent may strive to give his or her child the best they can, God's ideal family is a natural father and mother. Studies of crime data have shown that an American child living with one or more substitutive parents, was about 100 times as likely to be fatally abused as a child living with biological parents.

There are 40 million Americans (many of whom are young children) who suffer from a "genetic" disorder, where the sufferers have brittle bones which can snap for no reason. In

27

America America

other words, the fruit of the womb is not being blessed with health and strength. This is fulfillment of God's warning to those who would give themselves to idolatry. Right in the middle of the Ten Commandments, we are warned that God would visit the "iniquities of the fathers on the children to the third and fourth generation" of those that hate Him (Genesis 20:5). While the godless would protest that they don't *hate* God, the truth is that they love their own conception of their god but they hate *the God of the Bible* "without cause." It is the God who curses the fruit of the womb, who is abhorrent to them. They could never imagine that God would be so heartless. But God is not punishing the children for the sins of the parents (Ezekiel 18:1-5). He merely treats those who sin according to their sins. Those who obey Him will have their children blessed with health and strength, and those who hate Him will not have those blessings. The choice is ours.

4. They would contract diseases including consumption, fever, inflammation and extreme burning (verse 22). The medical profession is losing its battle against the onslaught of disease. Many doctors don't know how to confront them, reflected by the fact that a 1994 study revealed that each year over six million elderly Americans

America America

are prescribed drugs which are described as "inappropriate and dangerous."

Earlier we looked at the massive increase in prostate cancer among men. Look at the medical profession's analysis of what causes the disease:

"The cause of prostate cancer is unknown. Heredity appears to be a factor. Hormones seem to be another factor. Sexual infection may or may not have a roll to play. The most likely sources of the disease involve diet; however, nothing is certain about diet either."

Doctors are deeply troubled that the flesh-eating disease that starts with a cut, becomes red, burning and tender, then blisters and spreads like wildfire, could become another HIV. Already it kills 3,000 annually.

In an article titled "Drugmakers are scrambling for new weapons to kill 'superbugs'," *Business Week* magazine (August 1, 1994) said,

"To scientists and doctors who thought they had annihilated such bacterial killers as tuberculosis and staph infections a decade ago with antibiotics, what's happening in hospitals today is more frightening than a late night horror flick."

America America

The article went on to say how helpless doctors felt in the face of the killer bacteria, and of the 2 million patients "who get infections in hospitals each year," up to 60% are struck by microbes that have become drug resistant.

5. The soil would not yield its blessing (verse 23). All food originally comes from the soil. Our meat comes from animals who exist because they ate grass, which came from the soil, etc. It seems that the FDA discovers something harmful in our food daily, from salmonella to bacteria in milk. Some farmlands of the United States have become so unyielding that they have been abandoned by farmers.

6. The weather patterns would work against, rather than for them (verse 24). The results of an average day's weather looks like a battle zone. Fires, often started by lightning strikes, rage in the West:

"The West's forest fire season which officially starts in mid-July and runs till October--is barely three weeks old. But already nearly 50,000 fires have burned 2 million acres, 700,000 acres more than were torched in all of 1993" (*U.S. News & World Report*, **August 15, 1994).**

America America

An incredible 220 fires were started by lightning in Utah in one week! Think of it--these are thunder and lightning storms *without rain*.

A new record was set in the first half of 1994. According to the Geo. Met. Data Service, there were 10 million lightning strikes in the U.S.--up by 20%. At one time there were a total of 22,000 fire-fighters battling blazes in western states. At that point there had been drought for eight years, and the Bible clears the sky of any confusion as to Who makes the rain:

"That you may be children of your Father who is in Heaven; for He makes His sun (note who owns it) to rise on the evil and the good, *and sends rain on the just and the unjust*" (Matthew 5:45, italics added).

The Scriptures also light up understanding as to who sends lightning:

"He sent out arrows and scattered them; lightning bolts, and He vanquished them" (2 Samuel 22:15).

The East and Mid-West are soaked sodden because of too much rain, destroying lives and covering entire towns, and the South is torn

America America

apart because of tornadoes and hurricanes. Other parts of the country who have never had them before, are beginning to get tornadoes and even earthquakes.

When I was a child, the healthy thing to do was get plenty of sunshine and fresh air. Not so nowadays. Experts predict that in the next 15 years, 12,000,000 Americans will get skin cancer. The world would have us think that this has nothing to do with the *Creator* of the sun but the hole in the ozone layer. God stands passively by, like the captain of a sinking ship with a hole in its hull. We are told by some that it is the hole which is causing the phenomenon of "global warming." A few years ago, the pseudo-intellectuals of the world told us the big threat was global *freezing*.

7. They would be given to insanity (verse 28). Psychiatrists are having revival with incurable diseases such as Alzheimer's, now afflicting millions in the U.S.

8. They would be given over to irrational fear (verses 28-29). Millions suffer from agrophobia and other terrors which often have no rational explanation.

9. They would have marriage breakdown, repossession, bankruptcy (verse 30). Millions have abandoned the institution of marriage, and

America America

of those who do get married, 50% end in divorce. The business market is so financially unstable, lawyers are having a field-day with repossessions and bankruptcy.

10. There would be national debt (verse 44). There is no point in recording the present national debt. It is increasing so fast, any estimate would be inaccurate within the hour. By the year 2000, every man, woman and child in the U.S. will owe $300,000.

Chapter Three
What's Going On?

Meanwhile, despite our national sins, a blind and mystified world points to everything from coffee to hot dogs as the reason for the increase in cancer. On a nationwide television program, a desperate host spoke of the alarming increase in breast cancer among women. When one woman said that years ago she heard that the chances of getting the disease were one in eleven, and now they were one in eight, the alarmed host asked, "*What's going on here!*" The show's guest "expert" replied, "That's what the medical profession has yet to find." She then suggested that perhaps the cause was in our diet, or because of the use of alcohol.

Perhaps you think that many experts are right in their belief that the cause of the cancer in-

America America

crease is too much fat in our diet. To deal with the cancer problem, Americans must cut milk, cheese, eggs, butter, meat, chicken and salt from their diet. Then, we need to drink more water and get plenty of exercise. If that's what you believe, then you will have to choose one fork or the other and then follow that avenue. Either you listen to the Word of God or the word of the ungodly.

Here is something to chew over:

1. The Scriptures tell us that God's blessing is "a land flowing with milk" (Exodus 3:8).
2. Jesus ate butter (Isaiah 7:15).
3. Jesus said that eggs are good food to give children (Luke 11:12-13).
4. God says meat is good and should never be refused (1 Timothy 4:3-4).
5. Jesus said that salt is good (Mark 9:50).
6. The Bible says that exercise doesn't do much good (1 Timothy 4:8).

If you follow the counsel of the ungodly, you may end up saying what Jacqueline Kennedy Onassis said as she lay dying of cancer:

"I don't get it. I did everything right to take care of myself and look at what happened.

America America

Why in the world did I do all those push-ups?"

The very word "cancer" strikes fear in the heart of the contemporary world. One by one their hopes are being stripped from them. In July of 1994, a study revealed that the regular use of vitamins was worthless in the face of the disease. Millions daily feed themselves with handfuls of vitamin C, E, and others they think are helping them fight off cancer, and all they are really doing is feeding a $4 billion industry.

Health experts have been in the past, spouting their belief that to be healthy, we should drink eight glassfuls of water each day, but of late, even that has become hard to swallow. One million Americans become sick through drinking polluted water, and 900 die each year. An estimated 50 million people drink water which is polluted.

As the blessings of God have been removed from the soil, the secular world thinks nothing of spraying crops with hundreds of thousands of tons of poisons each year to try and combat the onslaught of pestilence. The influence of generations of evolutionary philosophy has them thinking that they are merely assisting (a not quite fully evolved) Mother Nature. The thought that

America America

they have somehow offended God doesn't even enter the arena of godless reflection.

Even though the situation seems hopeless, there is a way to avert further judgments of God upon America. If we want to see a stop to the pitiful sight of children with leukemia, more terrible disasters, cancer and other horrible diseases from further flooding this nation, there is a remedy. There *is* a way we can, with the help of God, bring healing to this once great country.

Predictable Anarchy

To bring this nation to the point of self-examination, we must first show them that they have offended God by violating the Ten Commandments. To do this, we should understand that the Law of God cannot make a person right with God. It is merely a God-given mirror reflecting what we are in truth. If the Church would hold the mirror up for the world to see, they would become "convinced of the Law as transgressors," and see that the Gospel is their only hope of salvation, both individually and nationally.

At first we may think that God's Law causes something called "legalism," but it actually does the opposite. The Law produces liberty--that's

America America

why it is called "the perfect Law of liberty" (James 1:25). A city whose drivers are lawful has the liberty of flowing, problem-free traffic. But if drivers refuse to obey traffic laws, there will be accidents, pain and chaos. Winston Churchill was right when he said, "If a nation won't be ruled by God, it will be ruled by anarchy." We are suffering the consequences of Lawlessness.

However, the purpose of God's Law isn't solely to produce national harmony but to act as a "schoolmaster to bring us to Christ" (Galatians 3:24). Knowledge of the Law and its ensuing wrath upon those who transgress it, has a way of making us cling to the grace of God in Christ, in the same way that knowledge of the law of gravity and the repercussions of its transgression makes a man cling to a parachute. When the world is told of the "jump" it must take at death, and the fearful consequences of Judgment Day, their God-given will to live will make them desire to "put on the Lord Jesus Christ" and trust Him for their salvation.

The Paradox of Law

Take the man who practices what he sees as the virtue of restraint. He takes "Don't drink and drive" one step further--he doesn't drink. This isn't because he hasn't the liberty to drink but because he understands that alcohol is a toxin. He cultivates self-control over his sexual desires and restrains his appetite for food. To the world, he is a "prude," a puritanical goody-good, who is so bound by the rule of law, that he isn't free to enjoy life's legitimate pleasures. Yet in truth, this man has a firm grip on the reins of his passions. His mental state is clear, his marriage is solid, his body is healthy, and his children follow in his steps.

Now, think of the man who has the "freedom" to read pornography, soak himself in alcohol, and eat food to the full. He is the one whose marriage ends up on the rocks (according to evolutionary psychologist Douglas Kenrick, "men who are shown pictures of *Playboy* models later describe themselves as less in love with their wives than do men shown other images" Time, August 15, 1994).

He is also given to obesity, and his psychiatrist or physician has to check him into an alcohol or drug treatment center.

It seems that modern America will bend over double to shed any personal responsibility for her sins. Alcohol and drug addictions are called a sickness rather than a sin. If the drunkard is a drunkard through no fault of his own, then God

America America

is unjust in calling it "sin" and holding him personally responsible for the vice of drunkenness (1 Corinthians 6:10).

While each of us must feel a sense of pain when we see the fruit of gluttony when someone eats themselves into the grave, as in the case of the 34 year old woman who weighed 1,200 pounds at her death in 1994, we must remember that it was *her* mouth that let the food in. Ironically, the woman's tragic death came the same day as a report was released by the *Journal of the American Medical Association*, showing that Americans were more overweight than they were in the previous ten years and that millions had given up on daily exercise. Rather than acknowledge over-eating as sin and repenting of it, we have associations (such as the one in Sacramento, California), called the "National Association to Advance Fat Acceptance."

Accepting drunkenness, gluttony, and addiction to pornography, etc. as sickness, doesn't deal with the root of the problem.

The man who gives himself to intemperance often has his children follow in his steps. He lets go of the reins of his passions and finds he loses control of every area of his life. He refused to cultivate self-control and he lost control of himself. He served sin and became a slave to

America America

sin. One man finds liberty in law, the other finds slavery in vice...and the same thing happens to nations. Secular America has said of those who uphold what they see as the shackles of the Judean Christian ethic (the Law of God), "Let us cast away their cords from us."

The United States has moved so far from the moral Law, she can no longer say with those who founded her, "Oh how I love Your Law, it is my meditation night and day." A Colorado Court of Appeals ruled unanimously that a monument inscribed with the words "I AM the LORD thy God," had to be removed from a state-owned park across from the state Capitol. It was said to be a violation of the First Amendment.

Criminals and the Law

Above the doors of the Supreme Court building in Washington D.C. are the words "Justice, the Guardian of Liberty." Above those words sits Moses with the two tablets of the Law of Liberty, being clear reminders of the origin and basis for the American legal system. The Ten Commandments are engraved into the lower half of the oak wood of each of the doors of entry. The inner courtroom has panels directly above the bench where the nine judges sit. Inscribed on the

America America

panels are the words, "The Majesty of the Law," and once again the Ten Commandments. If the words "separation of Church and state" mean (as the world would have us believe) that the Church has no place in Government, then those who established this nation didn't know about it. Its original intent was to keep Government from infringing upon the liberty of the Church by undergirding the Fourth Amendment, which guarantees freedom of religion:

"Congress shall make no law respecting an establishment of religion, or prohibiting the free exercise thereof; or abridging the freedom of speech..."

A friend of mine recently visited a place called the "Carpenter's Hall" in Philadelphia. He thought that it was strange that a hall made by carpenters was part of the American heritage. A short time later, he discovered that the building was where the first prayer meeting of Congress was held, and the experience was so moving, a painting was done to commemorate the occasion and hung in the Carpenter's Hall. John Adams in writing to his wife, said of the opening prayer, "I must confess that I never heard a better prayer or one so well pronounced. It filled the bosom of

America America

every man present." In 1983, the National Park Service saw fit for some reason, to remove the painting and replace it with something they considered more appropriate.

Abraham Lincoln once said, "We may deceive all the people sometimes; we may deceive some of the people all the time, but not all the people all the time..." No doubt you are familiar with those immortal words, but did you know that that is not the complete quotation? He finished it with "...*and not God at any time.*" The world slashed the climax of what he was saying because it mentioned God and His all-seeing eye, *and that epitomizes what has happened to this once godly nation.*

As a nation, we have fallen from the grace that God shed upon us. We have turned our backs to God. *America the beautiful* is no longer beautiful. Violence and sin has made her ugly. She is reaping the fruit of her sins and it is time for her to be told:

> **"America, America,
> God mend thine every flaw,
> Confirm thy soul in self-control,
> Thy liberty in Law."**

What did the writer of "America the Beauti-

America America

ful" mean by "confirm thy soul in self-control, thy liberty in Law?" The answer is evident--as a nation we have lost our *self-control*, and from there we have also lost our liberty through *unlawful* desires.

Look at this impassioned plea from the Editor-in-chief of *U.S. News & World Report* (August 8, 1994):

"Three out of four Americans think we are in moral and spiritual decline...social dysfunction haunts the land: crime and drug abuse, the breakup of the family, the slump in academic performance, the disfigurement of public places by druggies, thugs and exhibitionists...there are the daily confrontations with almost everyone in authority: blacks against the white power structure, women against patriarchy, feminists against feminism, gays against homophobia, children against parents, mothers against matrimony, fathers against child support, churchgoers against church, students against universities. Instead of a culture of common good, we have a culture of constant complain. Everyone is a victim...gone are the habits America once admired: industriousness, self-discipline, commitment.

America America

"Personal impulses, especially sexual, are constantly stimulated by popular music and television, with other mass media not far behind. TV and music often seem to honor everything that the true American ethic abhors--violence, infidelity, drugs, drinking--and to despise everything that it embraces--religion, marriage, respect for authority.

"The nation's hunger for a public commitment to social and moral betterment is not a simple nostalgia for the greater simplicities of yesteryear; the clock cannot be put back.

"It is a profound and anxious desire to arrest decay. But if the dysfunctional trends continue, that anxiety will turn to fear, and even panic. And when fear comes to dominate social policy, reason and tolerance are at risk. That is our predicament."

America doesn't need "social and moral betterment." There have already been too many bandages put on festering wounds.

A morally "better" society would merely make America a nation of reformed murderers, rapists, adulterers, thieves, fornicators and liars, and would not solve our dilemma with God. His wrath would still abide on the nation.

America America

Bold Thunder

If all that is needed is a change for the better, then Jesus died in vain because we could deal with sin ourselves. Moral reform will not heal this nation of its scourge. It needs national repentance and faith in the One who can forgive our sins and heal our land.

It is only when the Church boldly thunders the Ten Commandments, to show this people their transgression, that this sinful and adulterous generation will come trembling to the foot of the blood-stained cross. It is only then that the wrath of the Law will be satisfied.

Confirmed in Self-Control

Look at how the fury of the Law is satisfied by the fruits of the Spirit of God, as listed in Galatians 5:22-23:

1. Love
2. Joy
3. Peace
4. Longsuffering
5. Kindness
6. Goodness
7. Faithfulness
8. Gentleness
9. *Self-control*

America America

Notice that the soul is confirmed by self-control. If godliness isn't crowned with self-control, a man will not be loving, kind, good, patient, and gentle, etc. A wife-beater loses control of himself--he loses his temper, he loses his patience, his faithfulness, his peace, etc. Self-control is the walls of the city that keep the enemy from taking control of the soul:

"Whoever has no rule over his spirit is like a city broken down, without walls" (Proverbs 25:28).

Then, after listing the fruits of the Spirit, we are told "against such there is no law." The Law of God is satisfied by the fruit manifest in the life of the Christian. There is nothing in that list that stirs up the wrath of the Law. That's why America must be driven to the cross by the Law. It is in Christ that the Commandments are satisfied and their fury appeased. It is when America is hidden in Christ that she will begin to be healed of her plagues, and by the grace of our God become great once again.

Time magazine recently published new findings about a lack of self-control in marriage and why it happens. It took nine pages of rambling to explain that the massive increase in adultery

America America

isn't man's fault, but a *genetic* problem. Man is merely an animal with inherited brute instincts. This is what the article said:

"The new science of evolutionary psychology shows why lifelong commitments are so hard for the human animal--and why adultery and divorce are so destructive...an emerging field known as evolutionary psychology can now put a finer point on the matter. By studying how the process of natural selection shaped the mind, evolutionary psychologists are painting a new portrait of human nature, with fresh detail about the feelings and thoughts that draw us into marriage--or push us out."

Why do so many men commit adultery? It is not *sin* in his wicked heart that drives him to do so, but "it is to a man's evolutionary advantage to sow his seeds far and wide." Men have the instinct to procreate and this often continues beyond their wives' ability to bear children, so their nature-given intuition drives them to look elsewhere.

The ramblings continue by saying that the problem is that adultery is undeniably destructive, so, although these instincts to sow seeds far and wide are given to us by nature, we should be

America America

aware that there are repercussions--

"Thus men might beware the restlessness designed by natural selection to encourage polygamy (adultery)...the danger is that people...will react to the new knowledge by surrendering to the 'natural' impulses, as if 'what's in our genes' were beyond reach of self-control."

Not only has experience taught him that infidelity is injurious, but he can't shake this cursed spoiler of fun also furnished to him by nature, his "conscience." The article ended with:

"Darwin himself believed the human species to be a moral one--in fact, the only moral animal species.'A moral being is one who is capable of comparing his past and future actions or motives, and of approving or disapproving of them,' he wrote."

That sounds familiar--"who show the work of the Law written in their hearts, their conscience also bearing witness, and between themselves their thoughts accusing or else excusing them" (Romans 2:15).

Chapter Four
Let's Personalize

Here again is just some of the chaotic fruit of not keeping God's Law--murder, theft, rape, drug-addiction, alcoholism, obesity, fear, hatred, sexual perversion, racial prejudice, greed, disease, spousal abuse, child abuse, child pornography, family break-down, etc.

Let's now stop talking about "America's" sins, and see how you and I *personally* stand morally. Answer the following questions with a tender conscience:

Have you ever told a lie? This includes any fibs, white lies, half-truths or exaggerations told in the past? Remember, time doesn't forgive sin. God sees the sins of your youth as though it was

America America

yesterday. If you have told even one lie, then you are a *liar* (be brutally honest with yourself because God will be on the Day of Judgment). Have you ever stolen something? The value of the item is totally irrelevant. If you have stolen one thing, then you are a *thief*.

Have you committed murder, or have you *desired to* by harboring hatred in your heart? The Bible says "whoever hates his brother is a murderer."

Jesus said if you look at someone and lust for them, then you have committed adultery in your heart (Matthew 5:27-28). Have you ever done that? Then you are an adulterer at heart. Have you had sex out of marriage, or committed adultery, or desired to? Then you have committed sexual sin and cannot enter Heaven (1 Corinthians 6:9).

Have you kept the Sabbath holy, always honored your parents, have you put God first in your affections, loving Him with all your heart, mind, soul and strength? Have you always loved your neighbor as much as you have loved yourself? Most of us have trouble loving our "loved" ones, let alone loving our neighbors. Have you ever used God's name in vain, either employing it as a curse word, or failing to give it due honor? Have you made a god to suit yourself and therefore been guilty of "idolatry"--making a god in your own image, believing in your version of what you think God is like? Have you ever desired anything that belonged to someone else?

It is vital that you listen to the voice of your conscience. If you were a doctor and you knew I had a disease that would kill me in two weeks, if you want me to take the cure, you must first convince me that I have the disease.

You will never accept God's mercy until you admit that you need it, and the only way to see if you need forgiveness is to examine yourself in the light of God's Law and look for the symptoms of sin.

A number of years ago, Cindy Zeligman and her five-year-old son walked into her kitchen and noticed a strong smell of gas. It was so strong she walked towards the door to go to her neighbors to call the fire department. At that moment her husband entered the room and told her to light the pilot light. Cindy protested saying that it would start a fire. He said, "No it won't," and lit his cigarette lighter to prove he was right. There are times when it doesn't really matter if we are wrong...this was not one of those times. He caused an explosion; a fireball which terribly burned 27% of his child's body, and 90% of his wife's body, putting her in the intensive care unit

America America

for two and a half months.

There are times in life when you and I make decisions that prove to be wrong. We learn a lesson and start again. But there is no second chance with your eternal salvation. The Bible warns, "There is a way that seems right to a man but the end thereof is death." You can't afford to be wrong. Don't light the match of human arrogance in the gas-filled room of God's holiness. Step back a little and think..."What if I'm wrong!"

If you have broken even one of the Ten Commandments you have sinned against God. On Judgment Day every sin you have ever committed will come out as evidence of your guilt. You will be damned forever and lose your soul. Without God's mercy you will go to Hell. The Scriptures warn that unless you repent, you will perish. Don't add self-righteousness to your sins by saying you are basically a "good" person. If you refuse to admit that "America's" sins are *your* sins, you will never seek God's forgiveness. Don't also think that God will forgive your sins because He is good. His "goodness" will make sure justice is done. He *will* punish liars, thieves, adulterers, etc.

Don't be fooled into thinking you can clean up your life. No "good" you do can wash away

America America

your sins--only God's mercy can do that. Two thousand years ago, He came to this earth in human form to take the punishment for our sins. The Bible says, "God commended His love towards us, in that while we were yet sinners, Christ died for us." When Jesus died on the cross, He stepped into the courtroom and paid the fine for us. His suffering death satisfied the Law you and I violated. The moment we repent and trust the Savior, God forgives our sins and grants us everlasting life.

That's how America can be healed of her plagues...God will overlook our sins because of what Jesus did on the cross. If you care about America, if you care about the children of America...if you care about your eternal salvation, tell God you are sorry for your sins, then turn from them in humble repentance. Don't put it off until tomorrow, you may not have that privilege--one in five Americans dies without warning.

Think of it this way--you are a man who has committed adultery. You have violated the trust of a loving and faithful wife. She is more than willing to forgive you, so how can you reconcile the relationship? You humble yourself, tell her you are truly sorry, then vow to never (even think of) committing adultery again. You

America America

shouldn't need someone to write words of sorrow for you to read to your wife, and you shouldn't have to read a prayer of repentance to God from this book. Just pour your heart out to Him. It's your *heart*, not the words that really matter.

Then put your faith in Jesus as your Lord and Savior. Trust Him in the same way you would trust a pilot with your life when you fly on a plane. He is but a fallible man, so how much more should you trust in Jesus. Read the Bible daily and obey what you read...God will never let you down.

Chapter Five
The Judgment of Sin City

There was a glint in the eye of the T.V. news reader, as she related how a massive Las Vegas sign was supposed to withstand 130 m.p.h. winds, and yet a storm had mercilessly torn it down and caused an electrical blackout that left 100,000 customers without power enough to gamble. She referred to Las Vegas with an appropriate name as she said,

"Sin city was ravaged overnight by a fierce storm which smashed a 362-foot, $4 million electronic billboard, leaving a 30 foot heap of twisted metal on the sidewalk."

The inference in the news item was that God had judged the gambling Mecca of the world,

America America

but of course, they weren't serious. This was merely colorful news script. Everyone knows God loves us. He would never be vindictive...or would He?

Did God lose patience with the pornographic industry, which has its core in Northridge, California, and send the 1994 earthquake to destroy it (as was suggested just after the quake)? Was He responding to a church's denial of foundational truths of scripture when a bolt of lightning struck and destroyed its steeple in England? I would like it to have been the finger of God, and I agree with the prophet's prayer, "Oh that You would rend the heavens and come down...that the nations would tremble at Your presence." I want the world to honor God. I want His name to be reverenced, and lightning tends to bring that about. After all, it *is* biblical. The disciples knew that God used lightning to judge sin in the case of Elijah, and asked if they should invoke a bolt upon those who rejected the Gospel (Luke 9:54). But Jesus rebuked their desire for Divine retribution, saying that it was born out of ignorance. The rebuke was not for believing in the principle of Divine wrath but for a judgmental attitude--Jesus didn't come to earth to destroy men's lives but to save them.

The fact is that God *was* on the other end of

America America

Elijah's lightning bolt (2 Kings 1:8-15). But, if we categorically say that every time lightning hits someone or something, or that when an earthquake strikes, these are incidences of celestial wrath spilling from Heaven, we open a can of intellectually difficult worms.

Take for instance the family who were out on a boating trip in June of 1994. They were struck by lightning and the whole family was killed. Were they into some terrible sin? What iniquity were the little children into, to incur such fury from Heaven? Why was that family struck dead by God, and yet Jeffrey Dahmer wasn't judged? He was the heinous savage who murdered, mutilated and partially ate eighteen human beings. Was their sin greater than his? Why do Christians get cancer and die in agony? If given the choice, some may prefer a quick transfer to Heaven by lightning. Why was a Chicago based Christian headquarters struck by a bolt recently? Was there sin in the camp? Maybe. Maybe not. Are the millions of lightning strikes each year all Divine wrath?

Is AIDS God's response to homosexuality? It seems to be very clear from Romans Chapter 1, yet if we say that everyone who has AIDS is the recipient of God's justice, then we can expect the godless reasoning of, "Well, He blew it,

America America

because over 2,500 innocent hemophiliacs have so far died from the disease."

A number of Jesus' hearers found themselves with this theological dilemma when they came to Him and told Him about the Galileans who had been slaughtered by Pontius Pilate, while they were involved in a worship service. They had obviously come to the conclusion that it was Divine fury working through the governor. Jesus refuted such a thought with, "Do you suppose that these Galileans were worse sinners than all other Galileans because they suffered such things? I tell you, no; but unless you repent, you will all likewise perish" (Luke 13:2,3). Then Jesus cited another hot news story of the day: eighteen people died in Jerusalem when the tower of Siloam fell on them. The accepted thought was that this was an obvious act of God, punishing them for their sins. But Jesus asked if these people were greater sinners than those who dwelt at Jerusalem. No, but unless His hearers would repent, they would also perish.

So, does this tell us that God pushed the tower over? Was Pontius Pilate an instrument of judgment upon the Galileans? Perhaps. Perhaps not. He used Nebuchadnezzar as an instrument of judgment upon sinful Israel. All we can gather from the Galilean disaster was that their sins

America America

were no greater than ours, so we had better lay our hand upon our mouth and make sure we are right with God.

Take for another example the shocking disasters that befall some of the nations around the world. Americans watch "live" pictures on T.V., of deaths of thousands of people through starvation. While there is a temptation for some to say the nations are cursed, that God has withheld the rain, that doesn't release us from the responsibility of God's Law. We are commanded to love our neighbors as much as we love ourselves, and even feed our enemy when he is hungry, so therefore we should do that which we are able to help relieve their suffering.

Although it would seem from scripture that particular retribution upon individuals and cities is very rare, such as the case of Sodom and Gomorrah, Annanias and his willing wife, the sons of Eli, etc., each one of us *will* be judged in the future. God's judgment is reserved for all unrighteousness. Sinful humanity is storing up wrath that will be revealed on the Day of Wrath (Romans 2:1-12). However, it is clear that when a nation is plagued by drought, hurricanes, tornadoes, disease, pestilence, etc., it is not enjoying Divine blessings but rather the opposite. If we are cloudy as to when God judges, we

America America

are in good company. This was Paul's conclusion as he began to wind down his Divine revelation in the Book of Romans:

"O the depth of the riches both of the wisdom and the knowledge of God! How unsearchable are His judgments, and His ways past finding out" (Romans 11:33).

Even though His judgments are above our comprehension, we can see that His dealings with nations are not entirely reserved for the Day of Judgment. The books of Isaiah, Jeremiah and Ezekiel give us insight into His judgments upon Babylon, Assyria, Moab, Philistia, Syria, Egypt, Ethiopia, Edom, Arabia and Tyre.

As we study the Scriptures, we can see details of the whys and wherefores of God's judgments upon His people. The Word of God was written for our instruction, to give us insight into the principles of Eternal Justice.

While we can't be certain about the details of God's dealings with the United States, as we have seen, there is a striking resemblance between Israel of old and contemporary America. Even if the pains that grip this nation are not specific judgments of God, we are still subject to certain unchanging principles of sowing and

America America

reaping. We have sown to the wind and we are reaping a whirlwind.

Let's take a closer look at the comparison of the sins of Israel with the sins of America, from scripture:

1. The Prevalence of Idolatry.
God said to Israel,

"What injustice have your fathers found in Me, that they have gone far from Me, have followed idols, and have become idolaters? Neither did they say, "Where is the Lord?" (Jeremiah 2:5,6).

Israel's prevailing sin was idolatry. Their hearts went after other gods. They knew the Law but transgressed its holy precepts because they didn't fear God. Even though God lavished His goodness upon them, they didn't seek Him or even ask why Heaven was silent. They sinned, and because there was no celestial reproof, they became bold in their iniquity.

God then said through the prophet,

"Return to Me, and if you will put away your abominations out of My sight, then you shall not be moved, and you shall swear, 'The Lord

America America

lives,' in truth, in judgment, and in righteousness."

Then He specifically warned the men of Judah and Jerusalem,

"Lest My fury come forth like fire, and burn so that no one can quench it, because of the evil of your doings" (Jeremiah 4:1-4).

Our God is a consuming fire of Divine yearning for justice. The mighty weight of Eternal Equity, like a giant dam of molten lava, towers over wicked humanity. It was grace that held back the dam from Israel and it is still grace which is only allowing warning trickles to wet the feet of sinful America.

God then puts His finger on the root cause of Israel's sins:

"For My people are foolish, they have not known Me. They are silly children, and they have no understanding. They are wise to do evil, but to do good they have no knowledge" (Jeremiah 4:22).

There is no other country like the United States. Its foundation is soaked in godliness. It

America America

was a nation established under God and yet we live in a generation that has no understanding. There is a form of godliness...an idolatry that conceives a non-existent god within the womb of its imagination. The god of modern America puts liberty above justice, its Constitution above Holy Scripture, religious tradition before truth, and mammon before God.

People still attend church in the millions. Over 95% believe in God but few love the God revealed in Scripture with the passion of those who founded this country. Despite the heritage, few say, "Where is the Lord?" because their lack of understanding has them thinking that God may be held at a distance, but it is the command to love God with heart mind, soul and strength that will bring them light.

If you study the works of the flesh listed in Galatians, you will see a strange bed-fellow couched alongside adultery, fornication and other human passions. Here is the list:

1. Adultery
2. Fornication
3. Uncleanness (moral impurity)
4. Licentiousness (lust)
5. Idolatry
6. Sorcery (Greek "phamakeia"--drug usage)

America America

7. Hatred
8. Contentions (quarrelsome)
9. Jealousies
10. Outbursts of wrath
11. Selfish ambitions
12. Dissensions (divisions)
13. Heresies
14. Envies
15. Murders
16. Drunkenness
17. Revelries (riotous)

This list sounds like a typical day in a modern soap opera (we are told by those who produce such programs, they merely reflect modern society--this is supposed to release them from all responsibility, as they don't feed vice, they merely reflect it as a neutral mirror).

Notice "idolatry" sitting in the midst. In the unlearned eyes of the godless, having your own god gives license to the rest of the sins of the flesh. They refuse to retain the truth about God in their knowledge, so they create a god in their own image to suffice the human need to acknowledge a Creator.

This is typified in the life of Hugh Hefner, the hero of much of secular America, who, in the summer of 1953, pasted his first *Playboy*

America America

magazine on the table of his kitchen. A loosely clad Marilyn Monroe was pictured on the cover. The bulk of the finance was provided by his strictly religious mother and brother, thus birthing the "celebration of sexual liberation." Here was the man who gave pornography respectability and placed it within reach of the common man. In truth, the bright spark ignited the first flame that has erupted into an inferno of lust that has ravaged and consumed an entire nation.

When interviewed on T.V. on the 40th anniversary of *Playboy,* he said that his magazine was an escape from Victorian morality--"In our society, we are more fearful of sex than we are of violence" (try and figure that one out in the light of 40 years of "liberation"). The entire interview was nothing more than an attempt to justify putting squalor on clean glossy paper, and the underlying spirit of the discussion was, "Here is the man who flew in the face of morality, and God didn't strike him dead. See, he did it. Time had shown that the 'God of Jacob does not see'--He has forgotten all about the moral Law. Hugh Hefner held up a light for more than a generation in the darkness of repressed prudity, so we can all follow his lead with a 99.9% certainty that God doesn't mind what we do."

America America

However, the .1% of doubt, like a small hole in a large liner, wouldn't leave the interviewer and Mr. Hefner alone. When "Hef" said that as a teenager, he put his first "pin up" on the wall of his bedroom to make a stand against the moral standards of his parents, the interviewer said, "...*like Martin Luther making his statement by nailing his thesis to the wall.*"

The interviewer then casually spoke of his own church, while Hef said that *Playboy* was a "time of Eden"--a sexual revolution. Suddenly, during the "live" interview, a studio light burst above the head of Mr. Hefner leaving him in darkness, provoking the interviewer to laugh nervously and say, "I hope this isn't an act of God."

2. Israel turned their backs on God as their source of life.

While we may not see this as a very great sin, look at how God categorizes the fruit of idolatry:

"'Be astonished, O heavens, at this, and be horribly afraid; be very desolate,' says the Lord. 'For My people have committed two evils: They have forsaken Me, the fountain of living waters, and hewn themselves cisterns--

America America

broken cisterns that can hold no water'" (Jeremiah 2:12-13).

In other words, Israel forsook the Lord and replaced His presence with other sources of sustenance.

Money is the god of modern America. When their hope for the future should rest on God, it rests on mammon. When faith in God should calm fears and give security, faith in money does it for multitudes. Money is loved with all of our heart, mind, soul and strength.

An insightful friend once said, "If the Queen of England was viciously assassinated, the networks would give it a few minutes on the news and then say, 'Now let's see how this will affect our economy.'"

But there is a terrible kick-back to this. The Bible warns that those who are given to covetousness (transgression of the Tenth Commandment) fall into "many foolish and hurtful lusts which drown men in destruction and perdition." When money is loved it produces all kinds of evil (1 Timothy 6:9-10), and pierces men through with "many sorrows," which is what we are seeing. What vice doesn't have its root in the love of money?

But there is still a wonderful hope for such a

America America

nation. The Scriptures say,

"Your own wickedness will correct you, and your backslidings will reprove you. Know therefore and see that it is an evil and bitter thing that you have forsaken the Lord your God, and the fear of Me is not in you, says the Lord of Hosts" (Jeremiah 1:19).

The hope is in the fact that America might find fear of the Lord and see that sin is an evil and bitter thing. This is discovered in the same way the Apostle of Grace found sin to be "exceedingly sinful,"--by the "Commandment" (Romans 7:13).

One of the fruits of Israel's forsaking God would be the influx of "strangers" who would devour their resources and the burning of their cities (Isaiah 1:7). From Florida to California, illegal aliens are breaking through U.S. borders and devouring assets, from health care, to jobs, to prisons, to unemployment benefits. California alone has over two million *illegal* aliens.

3. She became involved in nature worship

A reprobate society pictured in Romans Chapter 1, found that the door of idolatry always leads to the path of sin, and so when Israel

America America

turned her back on God, she ended up talking to the trees (Jeremiah 2:27).

In San Diego recently, a helicopter was not allowed to land to transport an injured boy, for fear of hurting the native forest in which the boy lay injured. Nature worship has replaced the worship of God for many in the United States, and nature doesn't care what you think of your neighbor. When a Californian woman was killed by a mountain lion in 1994, contributions taken for the lion's cub far exceeded those given to the family for the two children left without a mother.

When fire fighters were trying to put out forest fires in California, their helicopters were forbidden by law from fighting certain areas from the air, because they weren't allow to disturb the protected (and ugly) condor. Many, prize porpoises and whales above human life. A man was recently arrested in New Jersey for killing a rat. The rat was eating his tomatoes, so he trapped it and called the authorities. When the rat escaped from the trap, he killed it and was duly charged by the law. In California, a man was forbidden by authorities from farming his own land because they said a certain pest on his land was on the endangered species list.

A sinful society always ends up worshiping

America America

the creature rather than the Creator, then it pats itself on its pius back for its virtue.

It must make tree-worshippers gasp, in the smoke of the fact that Mother Nature burns her own trees by the million in forest fires (God Himself burns a third of the earth's trees in judgment [Revelation 8:7]). These were the same twig-brains who protested when loggers in Oregon cut down trees to provide a living for their family. They complain that this not only upsets the environment but it disturbs the protected spotted owl.

The godly are not blown along with such a wind of ignorance. They know that man is not just another animal that evolved on the face of Mother Earth, and therefore must yield to the rights of other species. They know that God created man and commanded him to *subdue* the earth (Hebrew: "conquer"), and "have *dominion* (Hebrew: "to rule, to prevail against") over the fish of the sea, over the birds of the air, and over every living thing that moves over the earth" (Genesis 1:28).

4. Israel was stained with the blood of the innocent (Jeremiah 2:34).

The soil of the United States is crimson with the blood of innocent children, murdered with

America America

the smile of civil law. God said of Israel that He didn't find the stain of blood "by secret search." In other words, their sin was blatantly apparent; as with the heinous crime of American abortion. Who would ever think that a woman could murder her own flesh and blood, but there are millions who have gladly done so and feel no sense of shame, and like Israel, add to their sin by saying, "I am innocent...I have not sinned" (Jeremiah 2:35).

A popular T.V. talk show host had a program in which his guests advocated the importance of having memorial services for miscarried pregnancies. When one woman held up a plaque with ink impressions of her baby's feet and hands the host said, "This is an acknowledgement of the value of this irreplaceable baby...this human being." Yet this same compassionate host is pro-choice; he is strongly in favor of the belief that abortion is a woman's right. His acknowledgment that a "fetus" is a baby, reveals that his pro-choice stand is wilful murder of a human being.

No longer can we excuse abortion advocates as ones who are in ignorance as to what they are championing. Neither can we continue to think that they are a small number with a loud voice.

A rebellious and sinful nation will turn to the

America America

devil before it will turn to God. Rather than crying out to God to heal the land of disease, doctors, in an effort to treat an epidemic of Parkinson's disease, are "experimenting with nerve tissue from human fetuses as a treatment." Hitler would have loved it.

5. Her sexual sin produced drought in the land (Jeremiah 3:2-3).

God fed Israel "to the full," yet they lined up outside brothels like an army.

"Therefore thus says the Lord God: 'Behold, My anger and My fury will be poured out on this place--on man and on beast, on the trees of the field and on the fruit of the field and on the fruit of the ground. And it will burn and not be quenched'" (Jeremiah 7:18-20).

Yet all the while, God held out His hand of mercy to them:

"But this is what I commanded them, saying, 'Obey My voice and I will be your God, and you shall be My people. And walk in all the ways that I have commanded you, *that it may be well with you*" **(verse 23, italics added).**

America America

The U.S. Surgeon General during the Clinton administration, Joycelyn Elders, reflected the thoughts of many with her insane, "We've taught our children in driver's education what to do in the front seat, now we've got to teach them what to do in the back seat." Elders said she wanted to see the day when every teenage girl carried a condom in her purse on dates...and when sex education was required for children as young as kindergarten.

6. Israel was given to godless judges, who did not exercise justice or truth (Jeremiah 5:1-3).

In 1994, a Presbyterian church in Florida which hosted a pro-life rally in 1989, was sued by the National Organization for Women under the new "racketeering law," a law originally aimed at organizations such as the mafia. The court sided with the pro-abortion women and ordered the church to pay the $291,000 legal fees. When the members of the church couldn't raise the money, the courts ordered that their church property be seized. This case was not exceptional. Courts throughout the land have become absurd in their attitudes towards those who stand against abortion.

America is far removed from the principles of biblical Law upon which its justice system was

America America

founded. To become an American citizen I had to answer a number of questions given to me by the Immigration and Naturalization Service. One of the questions was, "Why did the pilgrims come to America?" The answer was, "For religious freedom."

It is no longer a big deal to take the life of another human being, which is reflected in the penalties handed down by the courts for murder. The average life-term given to a murderer is 15 years, while the average term spent in prison is a mere five and a half years. Many spend longer terms in prison for financial impropriety.

7. Israel Increased In Homosexual Pride.

"The look on their countenance witnesses against them, and they declare their sin as Sodom; they do not hide it. Woe to their soul! For they have brought evil upon themselves" (Isaiah 3:9).

Hundreds of thousands of homosexuals march each year through the cities of America in "Gay Pride" week, to openly and proudly declare their shame. Even though they have reaped AIDS as a direct result of their lifestyle, with multitudes dying horrific deaths, they are neither repentant

America America

or deterred from their sinful course.

Jeremiah 5:3 says,

"You have stricken them, but they have not grieved; You have consumed them, but they have refused to receive correction. They have made their faces harder than rock; they have refused to return."

The Prophetical Mandate

Jeremiah was told what he was to say to Israel as these judgments came upon them. He was to boldly say that it was God's hand (Jeremiah 5:19). This is the mandate of the Church. We are to instruct the world as to why God's blessing has been removed, and not cower at the thought of telling the world that earthquakes, etc., are wake up calls--for the Church and for a sinful nation.

Yet, few are telling the world this message. As in Israel "...from the prophet even to the priest, everyone deals falsely. They have healed the hurt of My people slightly, saying, 'Peace, peace' when there is no peace" (Jeremiah 6:13-14). That is the message of the modern church. The message, "Jesus heals marriages, drug and alcohol problems, and fills the vacuum in the heart," has replaced the theme that God com-

America America

mands all men everywhere to repent, because He has appointed a Day in which He will judge the world in righteousness."

The word "wrath," among preachers has become rare. We have failed to warn the world to flee to the Savior. Many preachers are men of corrupt minds, "supposing that gain is godliness." They interpret the verse "How can they preach unless they are sent," with the word "money" on the end.

Still, the United States with all its sins, insists on lifting her head in pride and thinking of herself as a *great* nation, the only remaining self-made "Super-power."

It was Abraham Lincoln who said of America:

"We have preserved these many years in peace and prosperity. We have grown in numbers, wealth and power as no other nation has ever grown...but we have forgotten God! We have forgotten the gracious Hand which preserved us in peace, and multiplied, and enriched, and strengthened us; and we have vainly imagined in the deceitfulness of our hearts, that all these blessings were produced by some superior wisdom and virtue of our own.

America America

"Intoxicated with unbroken success, we have become too self-sufficient to feel the necessity of redeeming and preserving grace, too proud to pray to the God that made us!

"It behoves us then, to humble ourselves before the offended Power, to confess our national sins and pray for clemency and forgiveness."

Chapter Six
Creating Havoc

A bull is standing in front of you, a full 2,000 pounds of twitching muscle. His eyes flash with a fiery fury. Steam billows like puffs of smoke from his widened nostrils. Without a second's hesitation, he gathers his energy and accelerates towards you like a massive fire-ball discharged from a huge cannon.

You are horrified at the thought of being pulverized by the beast. Your heart pounds against your chest as terror widens your eyes. Adrenalin is being pumped into your system. At this point of time, you either have to run for your life, or you have to run at the bull and tear

America America

it into a thousand pieces.

It is a known fact, that to stand still and do nothing when adrenalin has been pumped into you, is said to be physically injurious to your body.

We are going to take a few moments to look at the fruit of men who knew the power of preaching future punishment by the Law. With the help of God they were able to effect nations. Once we realize the potential of what God has put within our reach, it should be injurious to our soul if we can read of these achievements and yet do nothing.

Two Strangers on Sandgate Street

It is very early on Sunday morning, May 30, 1742. The northern port city of Newcastle is still sleeping. Before church doors open, two strangers from London, one a thin man in his late thirties, walk silently down Sandgate Street in the poorest and most contemptible part of town.

They stop at the end of the street and begin singing the 100th Psalm. A few curious people gather and listen. Then the shorter man starts preaching from Isaiah 53:5. The small crowd of listeners grows to several hundred, then to over a thousand people. When the man stops speak-

America America

ing, the crowd gasps in astonishment. So the preacher announces, "If you desire to know who I am, my name is John Wesley. At five in the evening, with God's help, I design to preach here again." That night Wesley finds a crowd of 20,000 people waiting!

Wesley's journal reads:

"In the evening I reached Bristol, and met Mr. Whitefield there. I could scarce reconcile myself at first to this strange way of preaching in the fields being all my life so tenacious of every point relating to decency and order, that I should have thought the saving of souls almost a sin if it had not been done in a church."

From the time Wesley began field-preaching in 1739, until his death 52 years later, he travelled 225,000 miles (on horse-back) and preached more than 40,000 times!

George Whitefield was barred from London pulpits. In 1739, he preached for the first time in the open-air to about 200 coal miners. Within three weeks the crowds had mushroomed to 10,000 and it was then that Whitefield called on Wesley for help.

Perhaps his greatest meeting was in Scotland,

America America

where it is estimated that as many as 100,000 people heard him preach the Word. Many were bathed in tears for an hour and a half while he was preaching. It is claimed that 10,000 persons professed conversion to Christ under this sermon.

Whitefield had the God-given ability to capture the imagination of his hearers. On one occasion he was relating an anecdote about the blindness of humanity in approaching death and eternity. He spoke of an old blind man, tapping his way towards a huge precipice not knowing it was there. The old man approached the cliff edge unwittingly. Then, barely an inch from the edge, his stick dropped from his trembling hand. He leaned forward to pick up the stick...! Within Whitefield's congregation sat a dignitary named Lord Chesterfield, who was so caught up with the story that at that point he sprang to his feet and cried "...*he's gone!*"

General Booth, the founder of the Salvation Army had a brief creed--soap, soup, and salvation. Look at what history records for us:

"But for a long time Booth was too timid to hold meetings. Finally, after much time spent in prayer and the study of the Scriptures, he ventured to read the Bible and deliver some

America America

comments on the street corners of Nottingham. He was jeered at, ridiculed, and even bricks were thrown at him; but this did not discourage him. William's early efforts to speak in public were often very discouraging, but they laid the foundation of his future usefulness."

Charles Finney also caused havoc in the kingdom of darkness:

"Finney seemed so anointed with the Holy Spirit that people were often brought under conviction of sin just by looking at him. When holding meetings at Utica, New York, he visited a large factory there and was looking at the machinery. At the sight of him one of the operators, and then another, and then another broke down and wept under the sense of their sins, and finally so many were sobbing and weeping that the machinery had to be stopped while Finney pointed them to Christ."

In London, between 15-20,000 persons were seeking salvation in one day in his meetings. Enormous numbers inquired the way of salvation in New York and many other cities. The great revival of 1858-1859, one of the greatest reviv-

America America

al's in the world's history, was the direct result of his meetings. It is estimated that 600,000 people were brought to Christ in this revival.

At the height of D.L. Moody's ministry, one of his meetings in London was so tightly packed with people that Moody could not get in!

"...and there were still 20 or 30,000 people on the outside! Moody spoke to the great throng from the seat of a horse and cart, and the choir led the singing from the roof of a nearby shed! It is estimated that no less than one hundred million people heard the Gospel from his lips."

D.L. Moody said that the words that inspired him most were spoken by an evangelist that he heard in his youth:

"The world has yet to see what God will do with and for and through and in and by the man who is fully consecrated to Him."

May God enlarge our vision. The world has yet to see what God can do in America. This nation isn't too big or too sinful to be saved. Where sin abounds, the Bible says that "Grace does much more abound." Darkness only makes

America America

the light shine brighter.

All the nations of the world together are as but a drop in a bucket to God. He can empty sin out of the United States and fill it with a love for righteousness, in the same way He transformed Wales at the turn of the century ...there is nothing too hard for our God; with Him, nothing shall be impossible.

Chapter Seven
Let Lying Dogs Sleep

I felt good as I came out of a New York restaurant with three friends. As we walked towards our destination, I was brazenly approached by an unshaven street person wielding a cup filled with coins. When he lifted it towards my face, I gave a firm "No thanks." *There was no way I was going to take money from a man who was obviously in need himself.*

One can become a little heartless towards contemporary panhandlers, especially when you know that the pan they are handling is probably gold-plated. Some make up to $200 each day.

As we walked through the core of the Big

America America

Apple, I couldn't help but think how rotten it had become. Not only was it filled with crimes of darkness, but sin had become so overt. It was permeated with blatantly pornographic sex shops and peep shows, which had actually increased since the spread of AIDS. *Why had New York become so flagrantly lawless?*

A scientist once conducted an experiment to see if there were any visible signs in facial expressions when people lied. He had a number of medical students watch videos of the most gruesome operations imaginable. The students were then interrogated, and had to describe to the interrogators (who had no idea what they were watching), a most picturesque scene. The scientist then filmed the students faces as they lied, and came to the interesting conclusion *that human beings could lie well*--deceit came naturally to humanity.

His conclusion was fascinating, and seemed to confirm the words of Jesus in regard to identifying our real spiritual father, the "father of lies." The scientist said:

"What would life be like if we couldn't lie? If we had something that was equivalent to the dog's tail? Everyone would know when we were happy, when we weren't. What a terri-

America America

ble life; there would be no privacy! On the other hand, imagine a world in which everyone could lie *perfectly*, that everyone could mislead you without your knowing it. Basically the world we live in--where we can lie, but not perfectly--is probably the best."

Despite the scientist's self-deception, God sees his lying tail. There is going to be a resurrection of the unjust--He will not let lying dogs sleep.

The reason this man went so flagrantly against the work of the Law written on his heart, is because he had no fear of God. He seared his conscience, thinking he can transgress the Ninth Commandment with no consequence.

The great mass of secular society, including New York, thinks the same way--open lawlessness has become a lifestyle because they think there will be no consequence for their actions.

Take for instance what happened in July of 1993. The Washington traffic authorities made public a dilemma in which they found themselves. When members of a foreign embassy were issued with parking tickets for breaking the Law, because of their status, they were immune to any form of prosecution and therefore saw no obligation to pay for their violation. To that

America America

date, they owed the city of Washington, *six million dollars* in unpaid fines.

What happened? They lost respect for the Law, *and therefore, for the agency of the Law* because there was no fear of future punishment. They became bold in lawlessness thinking they would get away with their crime.

However, authorities came up with a scheme where vehicles which are driven by traffic violators would not be able to be registered, and they would therefore lose their cars, in an effort to force them to pay their debts.

The same thing has happened with the church. It has failed to preach future punishment for violation of God's Law; therefore sinners have become bold in their lawlessness. They have lost respect both for the Law *and for its agency, the Church.*

They are daily clocking up debt to the Law, thinking that they will never have to pay the bill. They are storing up wrath that will be revealed in the Day of Wrath. If on that Day they are found in debt, they will pay for it with their souls. Unless they are convinced that the Day of Reckoning is coming, that God will bring to judgment every secret thing, whether it is good or evil, they will continue to say that God does not require an account.

America America

Martin Luther, in his commentary on Galatians, wrote of what he called a demonic doctrine that was invading the Church of his day. He said that a "sect" had risen such as teach "that men should not be terrified by the Law, but gently exhorted by the preaching of the Grace of Christ."

His words perfectly describes the method of contemporary evangelism. It would never think of using the Law to terrify, but instead, in ignorance, gently exhorts by preaching the Grace of Christ.

Moved By Fear

L. E. Maxwell, Bible teacher and principle at the Prairie Bible Institute in Alberta, Canada, wrote back in the late 1940's of the fact that they kept records of students who came to a knowledge of salvation who were "moved by fear," and those who were "moved by love." He noted that between 1931 and 1949, of the 2507 students, nearly 65% were moved by fear, and only 6% were moved by love. The remaining 29% came with another motive or couldn't remember why they came to the Savior.

This side of Judgment Day, one can only surmise as to how those *not moved by fear* ever found a place of repentance. This thought pro-

America America

vokes the following inquiries:

1. What did they repent of?
2. When they understood they had *sinned against God*, did they not fear at all?
3. Did they not have respect enough for God, to produce the fear of the Lord which is the beginning of wisdom?
4. Did they not fear Him who could "cast both body and soul into Hell," when they realized that the wrath of God abode upon them?
5. When they repented, how did they "flee from the wrath to come" without fear?
6. If they were moved by the love of God seen in the cross, did they not fear at the extreme God went to *because of their sin* to redeem them?
7. As Christians, have they yet come to a point where they are "perfecting holiness in the fear of God?"

Understandably, Maxwell's silver hammer of conclusion was not a concern that so many had fled to Christ in fear, but that some didn't.

When F.B Meyer questioned 400 Christian workers as to why they came to Christ, "an overwhelming number testified that it was because of some message or influence of the terror

America America

of the Lord."

The famous Bible teacher then said, "Oh, this is more than interesting and astonishing, especially in these days when we are rebuked often for not preaching more of the love of God!"

A pastor who understood the importance of a sinner having a knowledge of sin, was once approached by his six-year-old son. The child said that he wanted to "ask Jesus into his heart." The father, suspecting that the child lacked the knowledge of sin, told him that he could do so when he was older, then sent him off to bed.

A short time later, he got out of bed and asked his father if he could give his life to the Savior. The father still wasn't persuaded of the son's understanding, and not wanting the child's salvation to be spurious, he sent him back to his room.

A third time the son returned. This time the father questioned him as to whether he had broken any of the Ten Commandments. The young boy didn't think he had. When he was asked if he had lied, the child said he hadn't. The father thought for a moment, then asked him how many lies he had to tell to be a liar, and when it was established that one lie made the person a liar, the child thought for a moment, realized he had lied, then broke down in uncontrollable tears. When the father then asked him if he now wanted to "ask Jesus into his heart," the child cringed and shook his head. He was fearful because he now had a knowledge that he had sinned against God. He could now do more than experimentally "ask Jesus into his heart," he could find a place of godly sorrow, repentance *towards the God he now understood he had offended*, and faith toward our Lord Jesus Christ.

After speaking of the importance of preaching the fear of the Lord, L.E. Maxwell said,

"Is the majesty of the Moral Ruler to meet with no respect? Is the authority of His Law of no consequence? Is there nothing in God to fear? An effete dilettantism would feign tell us so. Nevertheless all history and Scripture and experience cry out against such an emasculated and effeminate theology."

The true and faithful witness fears God more than he fears man. He wants God's smile for dedication to the truth of the Gospel, and his devotion will be rewarded:

"...those who rebuke the wicked will have delight, and a good blessing will come upon them" (Proverbs 24:25).

America America

What is it that awakens a man--the good news that he may have a free parachute, or the bad news that the Law of gravity will spread him over the landscape if he passes through the door of the plane? It's his knowledge of the law of gravity and the fearful consequences of breaking it that make him appreciate the worth of the parachute. Without fear, he will not see his need to embrace it.

Dr. Timothy Dwight, the founder of Yale University concluded:

"Few, very few, are ever awakened or convinced by the encouragements and promises of the Gospel, but almost all by the denunciations of the Law."

Isaac Watts, the great hymn-writer said,

"I never knew but one person in the whole course of my ministry who acknowledged that the first motions of religion in his own heart arose from a sense of the goodness of God, 'What shall I render to the Lord, who hath dealt so bountifully with me?' But I think all besides who have come within my notice have rather been first awakened to fly from the wrath to come by the passion of fear."

Author and Bible teacher Paris Reidhead said these wonderfully wise words:

"If I had my way, I would declare a moratorium on public preaching of 'the plan of salvation' in America for one to two years. Then I would call on everyone who has use of the airwaves and the pulpits to preach the *holiness* of God, the *righteousness* of God and the *Law* of God, until sinners would cry out, "What must we do to be saved?" Then I would take them off in a corner and whisper the Gospel to them. Such drastic action is needed because we have Gospel-hardened a generation of sinners by telling them *how* to be saved before they have any understanding why they *need* to be saved.

"Don't use John 3:16. Why? Because you tell a sinner how to be saved before he has realized that he needs to be saved. What you have done is Gospel-hardened him. What we have done in America is to Gospel-harden a generation of sinners by telling them *how* before they have any understanding as to *why* they need to be saved."

When we are true and faithful witnesses preaching the whole counsel of God, all we do is

America America

make straight the way of the Lord. We prepare the way of the Holy Spirit to convince men of sin.

Another author and Bible teacher, Walter Chantry said,

"The absence of God's holy Law from modern preaching is perhaps as responsible as any other factor for the evangelistic impotence of our churches and missions. Only by the light of the Law can the vermin of sin in the heart be exposed. Satan has effectively used a very clever device to silence the Law which is needed as an instrument to bring perishing men to Christ. He has suggested that the Law and love are irreconcilable enemies; they are opposites. If they are in conflict, men will obviously choose love and spurn Law; for no one would dare to despise love. Thus, the Wicked One has declared that love is independent of Law and contrary to it.

"Precisely the opposite is declared by Holy Scripture. Law and love are mutually affinative. Jesus plainly taught that the Law was urging men to nothing but love. The righteous commandments may be summarized as:

Thou shalt love the Lord thy God with all thy

America America

heart, and with all thy soul, and with all thy mind. And thou shalt love thy neighbor as thyself. On these two Commandments hang all the Law and the prophets **(Matthew 22:37-40).**

"It is imperative that preachers of today learn how to declare the spiritual Law of God; for, until we learn how to wound consciences, we shall have no wounds to bind with Gospel bandages."

John Newton (who wrote the hymn "Amazing Grace") said, "Ignorance of the nature and design of the Law is at the bottom of most religious mistakes."

If we want America to be saved, it is vital that we understand the difference of preaching future punishment by the Law, from what is commonly called "Hell-fire" preaching. When we preach the Law, we appeal to the "reason" of sinners. When Paul *reasoned* with Felix to a point where the Governor trembled, there is no hint that the Apostle merely screamed, "You're gonna burn!" Instead, he appealed to his common sense by speaking of righteousness, temperance and judgment; and the righteousness he spoke of was obviously the righteousness which is of the Law. This was spoken of in conjunction

America America

with judgment by the Law and this is why Charles Spurgeon said, "I do not believe that any man can preach the Gospel who does not preach the Law."

While the Church remains in ignorance of God's Law, in its capacity both evangelically and in its ability to produce and maintain the fear of the Lord in the life of the believer, it is being robbed of great blessing. In Psalm 94, the Psalmist speaks of God's justice, the sinner's ignorance, then scripture says, "Blessed is the man You instruct, O Lord, and teach out of Your Law."

Wesley said to those who didn't understand the Law's purpose:

"O take knowledge what satan hath gained over thee; and, for the time to come, never think or speak lightly of, much less dress up as a scarecrow, this blessed instrument of the Grace of God. Yea, love and value it for the sake of Him from whom it came, and of Him to whom it leads. Let it be thy glory and joy, next to the cross of Christ. Declare its praise, and make it honorable before all men."

Finger-lickin' Bad

On Tuesday, July 20, 1993, Donald Wyman,

America America

a woodsman in the back blocks of Pennsylvania lay helplessly under a tree that had fallen upon him. After giving up crying out for help, he saw there was only one thing he could do to save himself. He took out his pocket-knife and cut through his skin, muscle, and broken bone below his left knee.

As horrible as the incident was, who would blame the man for cutting off his leg that he might keep his life? Yet, rarely does the Church bring out before the world the great truth, "If your right hand causes you to sin, cut if off and cast it from you; for it is more profitable for you that one of your members perish, than for your whole body to be cast into Hell" (Matthew 5:30).

During the mid 1980's, a virus broke out in the chicken industry. The virus had the capability of completely destroying the industry, so they immediately killed 17 million birds at a total cost of $70 million. The radical step came about because they saw the terrible damage that would come if they didn't cut their losses. But that is mere chicken feed to the human loss that there will be on Judgment Day, because the Church thinks lightly of the disease of sin.

Chapter Eight
Fixing the Feet in Fetters

Can a sower have any influence over the type of soil on which he sows his seed? The answer is an obvious "Yes." He *cannot* have influence over the seed--that's God's concern. He made the seed and He alone can make it germinate, but a wise sower will do what he can to make that process easier, and take the time to prepare the soil *if he wants a good crop*.

The Parable of the Sower tells us that the sower sows the seed of the "Word of God" (Luke 8:11). The *Word* is the Greek word "logos," or the "spoken" word of God, specifically the Gospel of Salvation--"But the Word of the Lord endures forever. And this is the word which by the Gospel is preached unto you" (1

America America

Peter 1:25). It is the *Gospel* we are commanded to preach to "every creature" (Mark 16:15). Scripture tells us that it is the *Gospel*, not the Law that saves, it is the "power of God unto salvation" (Romans 1:16).

So the "seed" sown by the evangelist (the *preacher of the Gospel*) is the Gospel itself. Over this seed he has no influence--this is the incorruptible seed of the Word of God. One may sow, another may reap, but it is *God* who "gives the increase;" He alone generates the seed to growth. The regeneration of a soul through the power of the Gospel is *solely* the prerogative of the Spirit of God.

To look further into this, we will look closely at a number of thoughts from Charles Spurgeon, the Prince of Preachers. He said of the sower:

"His object was a limited one. He did not go forth to make the seed grow. No, that was beyond his power; he went forth to sow. If we were responsible for the effect of the Gospel upon the hearts of men, we should be in a sorry plight indeed: but we are only responsible for the sowing of the good seed."

However, as with the sower of natural seed, if the preacher wants a good harvest, he will

America America

take the time to prepare the soil of the ground upon which he is to sow. This is the next point to which he addresses himself as he continues to teach on the Parable of the Sower:

"Oh, that the Holy Spirit would drive the great steam-plow through you, and break you in pieces! It would be the happiest thing that could happen to you, though your misery might be deep, and your anguish terrible. And then may He sow you with His own good seed, that you may bring forth fruit to life eternal, having in this life joy, peace, restfulness, usefulness, and in the world to come life everlasting!"

Spurgeon says it is the "steam-plow" that the Holy Spirit uses to prepare the soil of the sinner's heart. What then is this tool? Here is his answer:

"But, my dear hearers, may God give you to have so much depth of earth that you may be pricked in your hearts, and may be weighed down with a sense of your own sinfulness! May the great steam-plow of the Law go right through the rock that lies at the bottom of your heart! May God's almighty grace change

America America

the rock into good, friable soil, which will be suitable to the good seed!"

The Law of God in the hand of the preacher is the "plow" the Holy Spirit uses to break up the soil of the human heart. It is *the Law* that uncovers the stones of sin which hinder the planting of the seed of the Gospel. Spurgeon now becomes more specific in the use of the plow:

"One other reason why this soil was so uncongenial was that *it was totally unprepared for the seed*. There had been no plowing before the seed was sown, and no harrowing afterwards. He that sows without a plow may reap without a sickle. He who preaches the Gospel without preaching the Law may hold all the results of it in his hand, and there will be little for him to hold.

"Robbie Flockhart, when he preached in the streets of Edinburgh used to say, 'You must preach the Law, for the Gospel is a silken thread, and you cannot get it into the hearts of men unless you have made a way for it with a sharp needle; the sharp needle of the Law will pull the silken thread of the Gospel after it.' There must be plowing before there

is sowing if there is to be reaping after the sowing."

The disaster of most of our twentieth century sowing of the seed of the Gospel (particularly in the United States), is that we have failed to see the necessity of preparing the soil with the Law. Consequently, we have masses in our churches who have been misled into thinking they are saved when they have never come to a place of "repentance unto life."

This was even the case in Spurgeon's day. There were ones who refused to yield to the scriptural example of, Law to the proud and Grace to the humble. Biblical evangelism is *shatter the hard heart with the Law, and mend the broken one with the Gospel.*

Here are Charles Spurgeon's thoughts on how the "evil" of having false converts in the midst of God's people could be avoided:

"In the case of the seed upon the rocky ground, there was, also, *a deficiency of sensitive vitality*. The seed grew for a time, and then became dry; and are there not multitudes of people, in our churches now, who are just like that? They are as dry as old hay, they have withered away. We cannot turn them

America America

out; but, oh, that we could turn life into them! Oh, that the water of life might bring forth fruit unto God!

"I have said enough, if God shall bless it, to set many people searching their hearts to see whether this sacred moisture is there.

"Now, to close, we are to consider how this evil is to be avoided.

"Well, first, let us one and all *cry to God to break up the rock*. Rock, rock, rock, wilt thou never break? We may scatter the seed upon you, but nothing will come of it till that rock is broken. The great steam-plow needs to be driven right through men's hearts till they are torn in sunder, and the old rock of nature is ground to powder, made friable, and turned into good soil."

George Whitefield had the same battle with unbiblical preaching in his day when he said:

"That is the reason we have so many 'mushroom' converts...because their stony ground is not plowed up; they have not got a conviction of the Law."

In his instruction as to the importance of soil preparation, Spurgeon says:

"Next, *the truly penitent gives glory to the righteousness of God in His Law*. The man that really hates sin says, 'Lord, I do not quarrel with Thy Law. Thy Law is holy, and just, and good: the fault is with me, for I am carnal, sold under sin. No law could be more exactly right and just that Thy Law is, and in having transgressed against it I am deeply guilty, and I own my folly and crime. Whatever becomes of me, I dare not impugn the Law which condemns me. I adore its infinite majesty and purity.' Impenitence rails at the Law as too severe, speaks of transgression as a trifle, and of future punishment as cruelty; but the truly repentant soul admires the Law, and champions it even against its own self. Do you know all this in your own heart?....Has the Spirit of God ever so wrought in you as a spirit of bondage, shutting you up in prison under the Law, fixing your hands in handcuffs and your feet in fetters, putting you in the stocks and leaving you there?"

Freedom from Legalism

The Apostle Paul says that the believer in Jesus is legally dead in Christ (Colossians 3:3). That judicial death is to the Law of God (Galatians 2:19). If that is true, why is it that the Law is actually hidden beneath the commands of the Apostle. If we are free from the Law, why are we told to deal with the following sins (Colossians 3:1-9):

1. Fornication, uncleanness (both mean a moral impurity and are a transgression of the 7th Commandment)
2. Inordinate affection (1st and 2nd Commandments)
3. Evil concupiscence (lust--7th Commandment)
4. Covetousness, which is idolatry (2nd and 10th Commandments)
5. Anger, wrath, malice (6th Commandment)
6. Blasphemy (3rd Commandment)
7. Lie not (9th Commandment).

If we are free from the Law, how then can Paul preach a camouflaged obedience to the Law?

Imagine if a man had a wayward son who grievously broke the Law. If he couldn't settle a $200,000 fine, he would be forced to serve a long prison sentence. When the son can't pay the fine, he is cast into prison.

His father sells his house and his car to raise the money to pay the fine, leaving him destitute. His son is overwhelmed, and broken in heart that

America America

his father would do such a thing for him.

What now should the son's attitude be to the law? Will he continue to be a law-breaker? No. If he has truly seen his father's love demonstrated to him, he will now obey the law in the light of his father's sacrifice. This isn't because he owes the law anything-- that was completely satisfied by the sacrifice of the father. His motivation is one of love and gratitude.

Here now is the Christian's attitude to the Law:

"Wherefore my brethren, you are become dead to the Law by the body of Christ (there is the father's sacrifice); that you should be married to another, even to Him who is raised from the dead, that we should bring forth fruit unto God" (Romans 7:4).

We are legally dead to the Law because of the sacrifice of Calvary. Christ redeemed us from the curse of the Law being made a curse for us. Now, like the wayward son, we live a *lawful* life, not because we are in debt to the Law but because we are dead to the Law by the body of Christ--it was satisfied in the Savior's death. We can walk free from the courtroom and even smile at the Judge as we leave. The Law

America America

has no condemnation to those who are in Christ Jesus (Romans 8:1). We have seen the sacrifice of the Father, so we live to please Him motivated by love and gratitude. We "bring forth fruit unto God" because "love is the fulfilling of the Law."

This is no doubt what Paul meant when he said he was "not without Law to God, but under the Law to Christ" (1 Corinthians 9:21). The Christian is free in Jesus but his is a *lawful* liberty. He doesn't use his liberty for an "occasion of the flesh."

Why then are there so many who profess to love God, yet use their liberty for an opportunity to sin? The answer is a paradox. The use of the Law evangelically (preceding conversion), produces in the believer freedom from the Law *after* conversion. A failure to use the Law preceding the message of the cross, will produce legalism and antinomianism (the sinning "Christian") in the professing convert after his commitment.

In his unregenerate state, the unenlightened sinner thinks that God approves of his good works. His corrupted mind concludes that somehow his good deeds cancel out his many sins. In his darkness, he goes about to establish his own righteousness, being ignorant of the righteous-

America America

ness which is of God. Like the rich young ruler, he boasts of his works (Luke 18:18).

But when the faithful Gospel preacher draws back the curtain from the Holy of Holies, and reveals the sheer brilliance of the Law of God, he suddenly sees himself in truth, that he is an unclean thing in the sight of his God and all his good deeds are as filthy leprous rags. As with the rich young ruler, the Law stops his mouth and opens his eyes. Like a guilty criminal who has overwhelming evidence stacked up against him, he dare not open his mouth. Any thought of justification leaves the guilty sinner's mind. His head hangs low before the Judge of the universe. This is the true work of the Law--to show us that sin is "exceedingly sinful."

Now watch the defenseless criminal as Grace appears. See him look in unbelief as the Judge dismisses his case in the light of Calvary's cross. He is free to leave the courtroom because of the Grace of God in Christ. The Law stripped him of his robes of self-righteousness before the cross, *and that same knowledge stops him from ever slipping into those filthy garments again*. He knows that he was saved from the wrath of the Law solely by Grace without works, and now he lives and breathes by that same Grace of God. *The Law killed any thought that his works com-*

America America

mend him to God. Even a lifetime of good works are performed as an "unprofitable servant," whose duty is his "reasonable service."

However, those who are not "dressed down" by the Law, i.e. they are not stripped of their squalid robes of self-righteousness and nailed to the cross by the Law, will partake of the Grace of God still thinking in their ignorance that their works somehow are approved by God. Like the woman who transgressed the Law through adultery, they are not left condemned and undone, shut up under the Law, hungering and thirsting for the righteousness of Christ. Their breath of life is not in the blood of the cross. They don't *cleave* to the Savior for their very existence.

When Paul spoke of being free, it was not a freedom *to* sin but a freedom *from* sin. He said, "Being made free from sin, you have become servants of righteousness" (Romans 6:18). The Christian is free in Jesus, but his freedom is so that he may now be a "servant of God," he will therefore have "fruit to holiness, and to the end, everlasting life" (Romans 6:22).

Chapter Nine
Fish With Fancy Fins

A pastor in Florida pulled into a gas station and felt the tug of God's Spirit to witness to the man that served him. He shrugged off the thought because there were other customers, so he made his way back to his car. As he sat in the vehicle, once again he felt an urge to warn the man, and share the Gospel with him. He felt that he should at least go back and give the man a tract, but instead he prayed that God would "send a laborer across the man's path." Then the pastor drove off and didn't give the incident another thought. That is, until he was told that the man in the gas station, closed up shop some time later, went home and committed suicide.

We can no longer afford to shrug off the

America America

prompting of our conscience or the prodding of God's Spirit. We live in the closing hours of time, when a generation is closing up shop and committing suicide.

Sinning "Saints"

I have always felt uncomfortable when Christians have quoted 2 Chronicles 7:14 as the answer to America's plight. Here is the verse:

"If My people, who are called by My name, will humble themselves and pray, and seek My face, and turn from their wicked ways; then will I hear their prayers from heaven, forgive their sins and heal their land."

The normal interpretation of the promise, is that the Christian Church is called by Christ's name and therefore it is applicable to us. However, a Christian is one who *has* turned from his "wicked ways." If someone hasn't turned from his wicked ways, despite his profession of faith, he is not a Christian, he is a hypocrite--a "pretender" (1 John 2:4). The promise of 2 Chronicles is in fact peculiar to Israel, but its principle is applicable to nations who have access to the righteousness of God in Christ. God is rich in mercy to *all* who call upon Him. The message of repentance therefore should not be leveled at those who love God and walk in holiness but at the ungodly, many of whom sit in the pews of contemporary Christendom.

Fuel For Zeal

A true story is told of a black slave girl of the last century, standing in chains as lust-filled men bid for her body. Her delicate features destined her as a sexual object for the appetites of her soon-to-be owner. One man stood firmly in the crowd and out-bid every other buyer, to a point where he paid far above the expected price. The young woman was dragged to the tall man, and he was handed the chains to which she was attached. The slave dropped at his feet sobbing, and began hitting his legs with her fists in a pathetic attempt to show how ashamed she felt at being bought and sold like cattle. It was obvious that this man would pay any price to fulfil his passions.

The man ignored her blows and bent over the woman, unlocked her chains with a key and said, "I bought you to set you free." The woman looked at his warm and loving eyes through her tears and dropped to his feet and held them. Her tears were no longer tears of bitter resentment, fed by misunderstanding, but tears of gratitude at

America America

such a wonderful display of lovingkindness.

Fueled by the distresses of this life, many of us have resented God. Yet, this comes by a lack of understanding. If God did what was right and just, He could have left us bound by the chains of sin and death. He didn't though. He bid for us and purchased us with the precious blood of Christ, and those who gain such glorious understanding, fall at His feet and become free slaves of righteousness. Such knowledge now fuels zeal to live for His good pleasure. How can we not delight to do His will...and *it is God's will that America be saved*. This is why Christ died--He is not willing that *any* perish, but that *all* come to repentance; therefore if we love God and love America, we will not hold back the charge given to us to preach the Gospel to every creature.

During the Second World War, a man and a woman met behind German lines. They were spies. The man couldn't understand how the woman could spy for the allies without a monetary incentive. He was an informant because his business would have been taken from him if he refused to cooperate, but she was motivated because of the injustice she saw in Germany. With tears in her eyes, she spoke of an empathy she found in her heart when she saw someone being viciously beaten by the Nazis. She said

America America

"suddenly, he becomes your brother."

Some time later, the man saw a group of Polish workers on a sit-down strike at a German oil refinery. The Nazis threatened the near-starving workers and then took one worker, and despite his desperate protests, hanged him on the spot.

The spy whispered to himself, "*Suddenly, he becomes your brother*," and from then on fought for what was right and just, rather than for selfish motives.

As sin seizes each American and drags him to the gallows of a godless death, empathize with his plight...allow him to become your "brother." Then let what is right, just, and good, spur you to greater heights of courage for your God--fight the good fight of faith until America is saved.

When the *Titanic* descended into the icy waters of the Atlantic killing over 1200 people, an official investigation pointed its finger at a man who captained a ship, which was close to the disaster but didn't respond to help. Apparently, Captain Stanley Lord saw a distress signal, but for some reason failed to turn on his radio. If he had responded, many lives may have been saved. The Captain was labeled a mass "murderer," something which devastated him for the rest of his life. Can you imagine the remorse in the

America America

heart of someone who could have saved so many human lives, but because he didn't see the urgency of the situation, didn't respond to a distress signal? Perhaps his mind was on other things. Perhaps he thought it was merely some prankster playing with distress flares.

In the black darkness, a dying America is sending out a distress signal for help. *Do you see how serious the situation is?* Are you more preoccupied with your own interests? Are you going to respond, or do you think you should rest your weary head on the pillow of apathy?

Compassion will weep for dying children in Africa, but *empathy* will send a check. Weep for America...but then put legs to your prayers. Calvary issued out of Gethsemane. Pray. Sweat drops of blood. Bear the reproach of the cross, and go into the highways and byways and compel them to come in. May we have the courage to lift up our voice like a trumpet and show this people their transgressions. *God help us with such a solemn task.*

* * *

We have many unique tracts, books, videos and tapes by Ray Comfort to help you be more effective in your witness (sample pack of tracts $2).

This book is available at very low bulk copy prices--call us for details on 1(800) 437 1893 or see the order form on page 122.

SUPER-SPECIAL: Buy our "Hell's Best Kept Secret" 16 audio tape series for $48 ($3 S/H, Canada $12 S/H), and we will give you FREE OF CHARGE five different titles of Ray's books, including *Hell's Best Kept Secret* (commended by Leonard Ravenhill).

EXTRA SUPER-SPECIAL: We also have a series of ten videos called "Excellence in Evangelism," for only $99.95 ($4 S/H, Canada $15 S/H). Buy this and we will give you ten different titles of Ray's books--free of charge. These videos are broadcast quality.
MONEY BACK IF NOT DELIGHTED.

   Send your payment to:

      Living Waters Publications,
      P.O. Box 1172,
      Bellflower, CA 90706.

Credit card orders 1(800) 437 1893
Fax (310) 920 2103

ORDER FORM for *America, America*

We trust you have seen the importance of this book's message. Why not bulk purchase directly from us, and give copies to your pastor, the church elders, the whole church, your friends, family, neighbors or congressman. You may even like to give it out as a tract.

Here are our very low price break-downs:

1-9 copies--$4 each ($2 S/H)
10-99 copies--$1 each ($5 S/H)
100-999 copies--80c each (5% S/H)
999-10,000 copies--60c each (5% S/H)

Credit cards 1(800) 437 1893
Or send your payment to:

> **Living Waters Publications**
> **P.O. Box 1172**
> **Bellflower**
> **CA 90706**